U.S. PRESIDENTS

The
United States Presidents

BENJAMIN HARRISON

ABDO Publishing Company

Megan M. Gunderson

visit us at
www.abdopublishing.com

Published by ABDO Publishing Company, 8000 West 78th Street, Edina, Minnesota 55439.
Copyright © 2009 by Abdo Consulting Group, Inc. International copyrights reserved in all
countries. No part of this book may be reproduced in any form without written permission from the
publisher. The Checkerboard Library™ is a trademark and logo of ABDO Publishing Company.

Printed in the United States.

Cover Photo: Getty Images
Interior Photos: Alamy pp. 14, 21, 29; iStockphoto p. 32; Library of Congress pp. 5, 9, 11, 12, 15,
     17, 22, 26, 27, 28; National Archives p. 25; Picture History pp. 10, 13, 19, 20, 23

Editor: Heidi M.D. Elston
Art Direction & Cover Design: Neil Klinepier
Interior Design: Neil Klinepier

Library of Congress Cataloging-in-Publication Data

Gunderson, Megan M., 1981-
  Benjamin Harrison / Megan M. Gunderson.
       p. cm. -- (The United States presidents)
  Includes index.
  ISBN 978-1-60453-455-9
  1. Harrison, Benjamin, 1833-1901--Juvenile literature. 2. Presidents--United States--Biography--
Juvenile literature. I. Title.

E702.G86 2009
973.8'6092--dc22
  [B]
                                        2008033504

Contents

Benjamin Harrison 4

Timeline 6

Did You Know? 7

Ohio Childhood 8

Family Man and Lawyer 10

The Civil War 12

Supporting Hayes 16

Senator Harrison 18

The Election of 1888 20

President Harrison 22

The Election of 1892 26

After the White House 28

Office of the President 30

Presidents and Their Terms 34

Glossary 38

Web Sites 39

Index 40

BENJAMIN HARRISON

Benjamin Harrison was the twenty-third president of the United States. He came from a long line of American leaders. Harrison was named after his great-grandfather. Colonel Benjamin Harrison had signed the **Declaration of Independence** in 1776.

Harrison's grandfather was William H. Harrison. He was a military hero who later became the ninth president. Harrison's father served as a congressman.

After college, Harrison became a lawyer. Then, he fought in the American **Civil War** before becoming a U.S. senator. In the Senate, Harrison established himself as an able speaker.

In 1889, Harrison became president. He served a single term. Harrison's time in office fell between the two terms of President Grover Cleveland.

During Harrison's presidency, six new states joined the United States. Also, Congress passed several important bills. One provided money for soldiers. Others tried to help American businesses succeed. After his term, Harrison returned to practicing law. He remained a popular public speaker for the rest of his life.

TIMELINE

1833 - On August 20, Benjamin Harrison was born in North Bend, Ohio.

1852 - Harrison graduated from Miami University in Oxford, Ohio.

1853 - On October 20, Harrison married Caroline Lavinia "Carrie" Scott.

1857 - Harrison was elected city attorney of Indianapolis, Indiana.

1861 - On April 12, the American Civil War began.

1865 - Harrison was promoted to brevet brigadier general; the American Civil War ended.

1876 - Harrison ran for governor of Indiana, but lost.

1879 - President Rutherford B. Hayes appointed Harrison to the Mississippi River Commission.

1880 - Harrison won election to the U.S. Senate.

1888 - Harrison defeated President Grover Cleveland in the presidential election.

1889 - On March 4, Harrison became the twenty-third U.S. president.

1890 - Harrison approved the Dependent Pension Act, the Sherman Silver Purchase Act, the Sherman Antitrust Act, and the McKinley Tariff Act.

1891 - Harrison supported the Land Revision Act.

1892 - On October 25, Caroline Harrison died; in November, Harrison lost reelection to Cleveland.

1896 - On April 6, Harrison married Mary Scott Lord Dimmick.

1897 - Harrison published *This Country of Ours*.

1901 - On March 13, Benjamin Harrison died; *Views of an Ex-President* was published.

DID YOU KNOW?

Benjamin and William H. Harrison are the only grandfather and grandson in U.S. history to become president.

The Harrisons were the first family to have electricity in the White House. However, they were afraid of getting shocked when they touched the light switches. So, they hired someone to turn the White House lights on and off for them!

Before becoming Harrison's vice president, Levi P. Morton was minister to France. President James A. Garfield appointed him to the position in 1881. After serving as vice president, Morton became governor of New York.

Benjamin Harrison was the last American Civil War general to be elected president.

OHIO CHILDHOOD

Benjamin Harrison was born in North Bend, Ohio, on August 20, 1833. Ben was the second son of John Scott and Elizabeth Irwin Harrison. John Scott and Elizabeth raised eleven children. The children were educated at home. Ben was a smart student.

Ben grew up on a farm called The Point. It sat on a point of land where the Ohio and Miami rivers meet. As a child, Ben liked to swim, fish, and hunt. He also did chores on the farm. Ben carried water and cut wood.

When Ben was just seven years old, he received exciting news. His grandfather William H. Harrison had been elected president! Sadly, President Harrison died just one month after taking office.

At 14, Ben went to Cary's Academy near Cincinnati, Ohio. There, Ben fell in love with Caroline Lavinia

FAST FACTS

BORN - August 20, 1833
WIVES - Caroline Lavinia "Carrie" Scott (1832–1892),
 Mary Scott Lord Dimmick (1858–1948)
CHILDREN - 4
POLITICAL PARTY - Republican
AGE AT INAUGURATION - 55
YEARS SERVED - 1889–1893
VICE PRESIDENT - Levi P. Morton
DIED - March 13, 1901, age 67

"Carrie" Scott. She soon moved to Oxford, Ohio. So in 1850, Ben began attending Miami University in Oxford.

In college, Ben was a good student. He studied Latin, Greek, and science. Ben also practiced **debating**. He gave wonderful speeches that listeners enjoyed. Ben graduated in 1852. He was fourth in his class of sixteen.

Ben was born in his grandfather William's home.

FAMILY MAN AND LAWYER

After graduating from college, Harrison moved to Cincinnati to study law. Then on October 20, 1853, he married Carrie. The couple moved to Indianapolis, Indiana, in 1854. That year, Harrison became a lawyer.

In Indianapolis, Harrison opened his own law office. His business grew slowly. Harrison needed to earn more money. So, he took a job as a court crier. In this position, Harrison made public announcements for the court. He earned $2.50 a day.

Harrison and his new wife lived in North Bend before moving to Indianapolis.

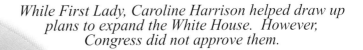

While First Lady, Caroline Harrison helped draw up plans to expand the White House. However, Congress did not approve them.

In 1855, William Wallace invited Harrison to become his law partner. Wallace was the son of a former Indiana governor. They formed the Wallace and Harrison law firm. Together, they enjoyed some success.

Meanwhile, the Harrison family was growing. Russell was born in 1854. In 1858, Mary was born. The Harrisons had a third child in 1861. Sadly, the baby died at birth.

Harrison worked hard to support his family. Mrs. Harrison cared for the children. She also volunteered in the community and at church.

THE CIVIL WAR

During this time, slavery divided the nation. Harrison was against slavery. The new **Republican** Party also opposed slavery. So, Harrison joined the party.

As a Republican, Harrison was elected city **attorney** of Indianapolis in 1857. Then in 1860, he was elected reporter of the Indiana **Supreme Court**. In this position, Harrison collected court **opinions** to be published each year. Harrison also continued to practice law.

Soon, arguments over slavery helped lead to the American **Civil War**. The Northern states wanted to end slavery. The Southern states wanted to keep it. In 1861, Southern states began leaving the Union. Together, they formed the Confederate States of America.

Indiana governor Oliver P. Morton

The American **Civil War** began on April 12, 1861. On July 1, 1862, President Abraham Lincoln called for volunteers to fight in the war. At the request of Indiana governor Oliver P. Morton, Harrison began **recruiting** soldiers.

Harrison entered the war as a second lieutenant.

Harrison bought a military cap and placed a U.S. flag outside his office. There, Harrison **recruited** many soldiers for the Seventieth Indiana Volunteer **Regiment**.

Governor Morton made Harrison a colonel. During the day, Colonel Harrison trained his men. At night, he studied battle plans. Harrison looked after his soldiers and was well respected. He was just five feet six inches (1.7 m) tall. So, his men called him "Little Ben."

The Battle of Resaca

In the military, Harrison learned to be a leader. In summer 1864, he led his soldiers in Georgia. There, they fought many battles leading to the attacks on Atlanta. These battles included Resaca, Golgotha, New Hope Church, and Peach Tree Creek.

Harrison then took part in General William T. Sherman's capture of Atlanta. Later, Harrison was recognized for his bravery at Peach Tree Creek. President Lincoln promoted him to **brevet** brigadier general. Then in 1865, the American **Civil War** ended.

The newspapers in Indianapolis praised Harrison's success at Resaca.

SUPPORTING HAYES

Following the war, Harrison returned to his law practice. He also resumed his job as court reporter. However, Harrison worked too hard and became ill. To recover, he traveled to Minnesota to hunt and fish. He then decided not to return to court reporting.

In 1876, the **Republicans** chose Harrison to run for governor of Indiana. He lost the election. Yet it turned out to be an important year for Harrison.

After losing his election, Harrison went on a speaking tour. He campaigned for Republican presidential candidate Rutherford B. Hayes. Harrison was an energetic speaker. He earned national attention for his work.

Hayes won the election. Then in 1879, President Hayes appointed Harrison to the Mississippi River Commission. This organization studied navigation improvements and flooding problems on the river. Harrison served in this position for two years.

Rutherford B. Hayes established the Mississippi River Commission in 1879. Today, the organization still studies flood control and other matters on the river.

SENATOR HARRISON

In 1880, Harrison won election to the U.S. Senate. Then, he and his family moved to Washington, D.C. Harrison soon became known as a good speaker and writer.

As a senator, Harrison supported **civil service** improvements. And, he fought for rights for African Americans. Harrison also believed the government should control the railroads. And, he supported a high **tariff** to protect American businesses.

Senator Harrison was popular among former military men. He supported many pension bills. These laws required the U.S. government to give money to **Civil War veterans**.

In the Senate, Harrison stood up for what he believed in. He spoke out against the Chinese Exclusion Act of 1882. However, this law to limit Chinese **immigration** still passed. Harrison served in the Senate for six years. He did not win reelection in 1887.

Senator Harrison

THE ELECTION OF 1888

In 1888, the **Republicans** nominated Harrison to run for president. His speaking skills, military service, and party loyalty made him an excellent choice. Harrison's **running mate** was New York congressman Levi P. Morton.

During the 1888 campaign, Harrison gave speeches from his home in Indianapolis. Nearly 300,000 people came to hear him!

Democratic president Grover Cleveland was running for reelection. His **running mate** was Ohio senator Allen G. Thurman. The election was unusual. President Cleveland earned more than 90,000 more **popular votes** than Harrison. However, Harrison

won 233 electoral votes. Cleveland received only 168. Harrison won the election! Rarely has a U.S. president been elected without winning the popular vote.

President Harrison was **inaugurated** on March 4, 1889. George Washington had become the first U.S. president 100 years before. So, Harrison was called the "Centennial President."

Harrison's inauguration

PRESIDENT HARRISON

As president, Harrison focused on foreign relations and supporting American businesses. In 1889, the first Pan-American Conference met in Washington, D.C. There, Harrison helped create trade agreements between the United States and Latin American countries.

In 1890, President Harrison approved four important bills. The first bill was the Dependent Pension Act. It provided money to **Civil War veterans** who could no longer work.

Another bill was the Sherman Silver Purchase Act. It required the government to coin more silver. This created more money for people to use. Silver miners supported the bill. And, many people hoped it would make **debts** easier to pay.

PRESIDENT HARRISON'S CABINET

MARCH 4, 1889–MARCH 4, 1893

- **STATE –** James G. Blaine
  John W. Foster (from June 29, 1892)
- **TREASURY –** William Windom
  Charles Foster (from February 24, 1891)
- **WAR –** Redfield Proctor
  Stephen B. Elkins (from December 24, 1891)

- **NAVY –** Benjamin F. Tracy
- **ATTORNEY GENERAL –** William H.H. Miller
- **INTERIOR –** John W. Noble
- **AGRICULTURE –** Jeremiah M. Rusk

Harrison (center) *with his cabinet*

Another bill was the Sherman Antitrust Act. At the time, companies that sold the same product could join together. This meant there would be no competition between businesses. Then, they could charge high prices for their product. Americans would be forced to pay these high prices. The act banned these **monopolies**.

Harrison also supported the McKinley **Tariff** Act. This law placed high tariffs on products from other countries. It protected American businesses from foreign competition. However, the added taxes made some goods more expensive. So, consumers did not like this new law.

President Harrison was in favor of conservation. So, he supported the Land Revision Act of 1891. It created national forests, which protected U.S. land.

Harrison supported two other bills that did not pass. Both would have provided more protection for African Americans and their right to vote.

SUPREME
COURT
APPOINTMENTS

DAVID J. BREWER - 1890
HENRY B. BROWN - 1891
GEORGE SHIRAS JR. - 1892
HOWELL E. JACKSON - 1893

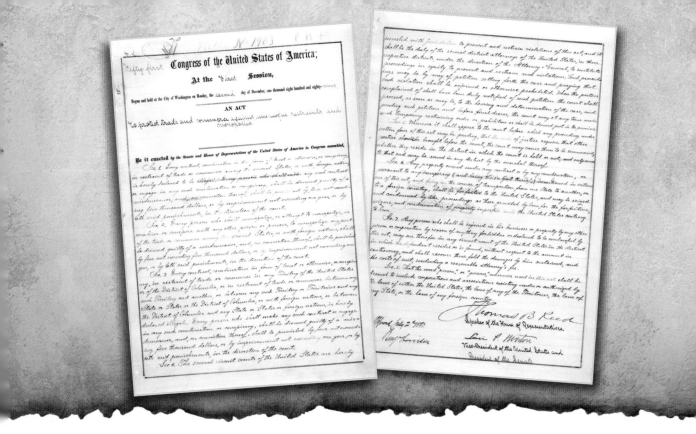

President Harrison signed the Sherman Antitrust Act into law on July 2, 1890.

While Harrison was president, six new states joined the United States. They were North Dakota, South Dakota, Montana, Washington, Wyoming, and Idaho. Also, land in Oklahoma opened for white settlement in 1889. Before then, it had been reserved for Native Americans to live on.

THE ELECTION OF 1892

In 1892, President Harrison decided to run for reelection. His new **running mate** was Whitelaw Reid. Reid was minister to France and editor of the *New York Tribune*.

The **Democrats** nominated former president Grover Cleveland. His running mate was Illinois representative Adlai E. Stevenson. James B. Weaver ran for the **Populist** Party.

Whitelaw Reid served as ambassador to Great Britain from 1905 to 1912.

During the campaign, Mrs. Harrison was very ill. So, President Harrison did not travel a lot to make speeches. Out of respect for Harrison, neither did Cleveland.

Then on October 25, Caroline Harrison died. Two weeks later, President Harrison lost the election. Cleveland won with 277 electoral votes. Harrison received 145 votes, and Weaver received just 22.

Grover Cleveland is the only U.S. president to serve two terms that were not in a row.

AFTER THE WHITE HOUSE

Mary Harrison

Harrison returned home to Indiana in March 1893. Then on April 6, 1896, he married Mary Scott Lord Dimmick. In 1897, the couple had a daughter named Elizabeth.

Meanwhile, Harrison practiced law and wrote. He participated in national and international court cases. And in 1897, he published a book on the federal government. It is called *This Country of Ours*.

On March 13, 1901, Benjamin Harrison died. He is buried in Indianapolis beside his first wife. Later that year, Mary published *Views of an Ex-President*. It is a collection of speeches Harrison made after his presidency.

Benjamin Harrison was a great public speaker. He supported conservation and defended African-American rights. Harrison is remembered as a leader who always stood up for his beliefs.

Today, Harrison's Indianapolis home is a national historic landmark.

OFFICE OF THE PRESIDENT

BRANCHES OF GOVERNMENT

The U.S. government is divided into three branches. They are the executive, legislative, and judicial branches. This division is called a separation of powers. Each branch has some power over the others. This is called a system of checks and balances.

EXECUTIVE BRANCH

The executive branch enforces laws. It is made up of the president, the vice president, and the president's cabinet. The president represents the United States around the world. He or she oversees relations with other countries and signs treaties. The president signs bills into law and appoints officials and federal judges. He or she also leads the military and manages government workers.

LEGISLATIVE BRANCH

The legislative branch makes laws, maintains the military, and regulates trade. It also has the power to declare war. This branch consists of the Senate and the House of Representatives. Together, these two houses make up Congress. Each state has two senators. A state's population determines the number of representatives it has.

JUDICIAL BRANCH

The judicial branch interprets laws. It consists of district courts, courts of appeals, and the Supreme Court. District courts try cases. If a person disagrees with a trial's outcome, he or she may appeal. If the courts of appeals support the ruling, a person may appeal to the Supreme Court. The Supreme Court also makes sure that laws follow the U.S. Constitution.

QUALIFICATIONS FOR OFFICE

To be president, a person must meet three requirements. A candidate must be at least 35 years old and a natural-born U.S. citizen. He or she must also have lived in the United States for at least 14 years.

ELECTORAL COLLEGE

The U.S. presidential election is an indirect election. Voters from each state choose electors to represent them in the Electoral College. The number of electors from each state is based on population. Each elector has one electoral vote. Electors are pledged to cast their vote for the candidate who receives the highest number of popular votes in their state. A candidate must receive the majority of Electoral College votes to win.

TERM OF OFFICE

Each president may be elected to two four-year terms. Sometimes, a president may only be elected once. This happens if he or she served more than two years of the previous president's term.

The presidential election is held on the Tuesday after the first Monday in November. The president is sworn in on January 20 of the following year. At that time, he or she takes the oath of office:

I do solemnly swear (or affirm) that I will faithfully execute the office of President of the United States, and will to the best of my ability, preserve, protect and defend the Constitution of the United States.

LINE OF SUCCESSION

The Presidential Succession Act of 1947 defines who becomes president if the president cannot serve. The vice president is first in the line of succession. Next are the Speaker of the House and the President Pro Tempore of the Senate. If none of these individuals is able to serve, the office falls to the president's cabinet members. They would take office in the order in which each department was created:

Secretary of State

Secretary of the Treasury

Secretary of Defense

Attorney General

Secretary of the Interior

Secretary of Agriculture

Secretary of Commerce

Secretary of Labor

Secretary of Health and Human Services

Secretary of Housing and Urban Development

Secretary of Transportation

Secretary of Energy

Secretary of Education

Secretary of Veterans Affairs

Secretary of Homeland Security

BENEFITS

- While in office, the president receives a salary of $400,000 each year. He or she lives in the White House and has 24-hour Secret Service protection.

- The president may travel on a Boeing 747 jet called Air Force One. The airplane can accommodate 70 passengers. It has kitchens, a dining room, sleeping areas, and a conference room. It also has fully equipped offices with the latest communications systems. Air Force One can fly halfway around the world before needing to refuel. It can even refuel in flight!

- If the president wishes to travel by car, he or she uses Cadillac One. Cadillac One is a Cadillac Deville. It has been modified with heavy armor and communications systems. The president takes Cadillac One along when visiting other countries if secure transportation will be needed.

- The president also travels on a helicopter called Marine One. Like the presidential car, Marine One accompanies the president when traveling abroad if necessary.

- Sometimes, the president needs to get away and relax with family and friends. Camp David is the official presidential retreat. It is located in the cool, wooded mountains in Maryland. The U.S. Navy maintains the retreat, and the U.S. Marine Corps keeps it secure. The camp offers swimming, tennis, golf, and hiking.

- When the president leaves office, he or she receives Secret Service protection for ten more years. He or she also receives a yearly pension of $191,300 and funding for office space, supplies, and staff.

PRESIDENTS AND THEIR TERMS

PRESIDENT	PARTY	TOOK OFFICE	LEFT OFFICE	TERMS SERVED	VICE PRESIDENT
George Washington	None	April 30, 1789	March 4, 1797	Two	John Adams
John Adams	Federalist	March 4, 1797	March 4, 1801	One	Thomas Jefferson
Thomas Jefferson	Democratic-Republican	March 4, 1801	March 4, 1809	Two	Aaron Burr, George Clinton
James Madison	Democratic-Republican	March 4, 1809	March 4, 1817	Two	George Clinton, Elbridge Gerry
James Monroe	Democratic-Republican	March 4, 1817	March 4, 1825	Two	Daniel D. Tompkins
John Quincy Adams	Democratic-Republican	March 4, 1825	March 4, 1829	One	John C. Calhoun
Andrew Jackson	Democrat	March 4, 1829	March 4, 1837	Two	John C. Calhoun, Martin Van Buren
Martin Van Buren	Democrat	March 4, 1837	March 4, 1841	One	Richard M. Johnson
William H. Harrison	Whig	March 4, 1841	April 4, 1841	Died During First Term	John Tyler
John Tyler	Whig	April 6, 1841	March 4, 1845	Completed Harrison's Term	Office Vacant
James K. Polk	Democrat	March 4, 1845	March 4, 1849	One	George M. Dallas
Zachary Taylor	Whig	March 5, 1849	July 9, 1850	Died During First Term	Millard Fillmore

PRESIDENT	PARTY	TOOK OFFICE	LEFT OFFICE	TERMS SERVED	VICE PRESIDENT
Millard Fillmore	Whig	July 10, 1850	March 4, 1853	Completed Taylor's Term	Office Vacant
Franklin Pierce	Democrat	March 4, 1853	March 4, 1857	One	William R.D. King
James Buchanan	Democrat	March 4, 1857	March 4, 1861	One	John C. Breckinridge
Abraham Lincoln	Republican	March 4, 1861	April 15, 1865	Served One Term, Died During Second Term	Hannibal Hamlin, Andrew Johnson
Andrew Johnson	Democrat	April 15, 1865	March 4, 1869	Completed Lincoln's Second Term	Office Vacant
Ulysses S. Grant	Republican	March 4, 1869	March 4, 1877	Two	Schuyler Colfax, Henry Wilson
Rutherford B. Hayes	Republican	March 3, 1877	March 4, 1881	One	William A. Wheeler
James A. Garfield	Republican	March 4, 1881	September 19, 1881	Died During First Term	Chester Arthur
Chester Arthur	Republican	September 20, 1881	March 4, 1885	Completed Garfield's Term	Office Vacant
Grover Cleveland	Democrat	March 4, 1885	March 4, 1889	One	Thomas A. Hendricks
Benjamin Harrison	Republican	March 4, 1889	March 4, 1893	One	Levi P. Morton
Grover Cleveland	Democrat	March 4, 1893	March 4, 1897	One	Adlai E. Stevenson
William McKinley	Republican	March 4, 1897	September 14, 1901	Served One Term, Died During Second Term	Garret A. Hobart, Theodore Roosevelt

PRESIDENTS 13–25, 1850–1901

PRESIDENT	PARTY	TOOK OFFICE	LEFT OFFICE	TERMS SERVED	VICE PRESIDENT
Theodore Roosevelt	Republican	September 14, 1901	March 4, 1909	Completed McKinley's Second Term, Served One Term	Office Vacant, Charles Fairbanks
William Taft	Republican	March 4, 1909	March 4, 1913	One	James S. Sherman
Woodrow Wilson	Democrat	March 4, 1913	March 4, 1921	Two	Thomas R. Marshall
Warren G. Harding	Republican	March 4, 1921	August 2, 1923	Died During First Term	Calvin Coolidge
Calvin Coolidge	Republican	August 3, 1923	March 4, 1929	Completed Harding's Term, Served One Term	Office Vacant, Charles Dawes
Herbert Hoover	Republican	March 4, 1929	March 4, 1933	One	Charles Curtis
Franklin D. Roosevelt	Democrat	March 4, 1933	April 12, 1945	Served Three Terms, Died During Fourth Term	John Nance Garner, Henry A. Wallace, Harry S. Truman
Harry S. Truman	Democrat	April 12, 1945	January 20, 1953	Completed Roosevelt's Fourth Term, Served One Term	Office Vacant, Alben Barkley
Dwight D. Eisenhower	Republican	January 20, 1953	January 20, 1961	Two	Richard Nixon
John F. Kennedy	Democrat	January 20, 1961	November 22, 1963	Died During First Term	Lyndon B. Johnson
Lyndon B. Johnson	Democrat	November 22, 1963	January 20, 1969	Completed Kennedy's Term, Served One Term	Office Vacant, Hubert H. Humphrey
Richard Nixon	Republican	January 20, 1969	August 9, 1974	Completed First Term, Resigned During Second Term	Spiro T. Agnew, Gerald Ford

PRESIDENTS 26–37, 1901–1974

PRESIDENT	PARTY	TOOK OFFICE	LEFT OFFICE	TERMS SERVED	VICE PRESIDENT
Gerald Ford	Republican	August 9, 1974	January 20, 1977	Completed Nixon's Second Term	Nelson A. Rockefeller
Jimmy Carter	Democrat	January 20, 1977	January 20, 1981	One	Walter Mondale
Ronald Reagan	Republican	January 20, 1981	January 20, 1989	Two	George H.W. Bush
George H.W. Bush	Republican	January 20, 1989	January 20, 1993	One	Dan Quayle
Bill Clinton	Democrat	January 20, 1993	January 20, 2001	Two	Al Gore
George W. Bush	Republican	January 20, 2001	January 20, 2009	Two	Dick Cheney
Barack Obama	Democrat	January 20, 2009			Joe Biden

"No other people have a government more worthy of their respect and love or a land so magnificent in extent." Benjamin Harrison

WRITE TO THE PRESIDENT

You may write to the president at:

**The White House
1600 Pennsylvania Avenue NW
Washington, DC 20500**

You may e-mail the president at:

comments@whitehouse.gov

GLOSSARY

attorney - a lawyer.

brevet - a military title given to an officer who has a higher rank than he or she is paid for.

civil service - the part of the government that is responsible for matters not covered by the military, the courts, or the law.

civil war - a war between groups in the same country. The United States of America and the Confederate States of America fought a civil war from 1861 to 1865.

debate - a contest in which two sides argue for or against something.

debt - something owed to someone, usually money.

Declaration of Independence - an essay written at the Second Continental Congress in 1776, announcing the separation of the American colonies from England.

Democrat - a member of the Democratic political party. When Benjamin Harrison was president, Democrats supported farmers and landowners.

immigration - entry into another country to live. A person who immigrates is called an immigrant.

inaugurate (ih-NAW-gyuh-rayt) - to swear into a political office.

monopoly - the complete control of a product, a service, or an industry.

opinion - a legal explanation of a judge's decision on a particular case.

popular vote - the vote of the entire body of people with the right to vote.

Populist - a member of the Populist political party. In the late 1800s, Populists supported farmers.

recruit - to get someone to join a group. A person who is recruited is also called a recruit.

regiment - a large military unit made up of troops.

Republican - a member of the Republican political party. When Benjamin Harrison was president, Republicans supported business and strong government.

running mate - a candidate running for a lower-rank position on an election ticket, especially the candidate for vice president.

Supreme Court - the highest, most powerful court of a nation or a state.

tariff - the taxes a government puts on imported or exported goods.

veteran - a person who has served in the armed forces.

WEB SITES

To learn more about Benjamin Harrison, visit ABDO Publishing Company on the World Wide Web at **www.abdopublishing.com**. Web sites about Benjamin Harrison are featured on our Book Links page. These links are routinely monitored and updated to provide the most current information available.

INDEX

A

American Civil War 4, 12, 13, 14, 15, 16, 18, 22

B

birth 8

C

childhood 8

Chinese Exclusion Act 18

Cleveland, Grover 4, 21, 26, 27

D

death 28

Declaration of Independence 4

Democratic Party 21, 26

Dependent Pension Act 22

E

education 4, 8, 9, 10

F

family 4, 8, 9, 10, 11, 18, 27, 28

H

Hayes, Rutherford B. 16

health 16

I

Idaho 25

inauguration 21

Indiana Supreme Court reporter 12, 16

Indianapolis city attorney 12

L

Land Revision Act 24

Lincoln, Abraham 13, 15

M

McKinley Tariff Act 24

military service 4, 13, 14, 15, 20

Mississippi River Commission 16

Montana 25

Morton, Levi P. 20

Morton, Oliver P. 13, 14

N

Native Americans 25

North Dakota 25

P

Pan-American Conference 22

Populist Party 26

R

Reid, Whitelaw 26

Republican Party 12, 16, 20

retirement 28

S

Senate, U.S. 4, 18

Sherman, William T. 15

Sherman Antitrust Act 24

Sherman Silver Purchase Act 22

slavery 12

South Dakota 25

Stevenson, Adlai E. 26

T

This Country of Ours 28

Thurman, Allen G. 21

V

Views of an Ex-President 28

W

Wallace, William 11

Washington 25

Washington, George 21

Weaver, James B. 26, 27

Wyoming 25